THE SPECIAL ONE
The Wit and Wisdom of

JOSÉ MOURINHO

THE SPECIAL ONE
The Wit and Wisdom of

JOSÉ MOURINHO

Compiled by

John Amhurst

First published in Great Britain in 2005 by

Virgin Books Ltd
Thames Wharf Studios
Rainville Road
London
W6 9HA

A catalogue record for this book is available from
the British Library.

ISBN 0 7535 1079 0

The paper used in this book is a natural,
recyclable product made from wood grown in
sustainable forests. The manufacturing process
conforms to the regulations of the country of
origin.

Typeset by Phoenix Photosetting, Chatham, Kent
Printed and bound in Great Britain by
Mackays of Chatham, Kent

CONTENTS

Everyone wondered whether he could actually, seriously, do it, whether for all the talk and the banter he would flatter to deceive. By Christmas, very few doubters remained. Chelsea were dominant, frequently brilliant, and were on course for an unprecedented four trophies. That they didn't win all of them, Mourinho would probably argue, was unlucky.

Throughout that first season, Mourinho remained entertaining, aloof, occasionally infuriating, but always beguiling. He made the rest of the managers seem ordinary by comparison. Ferguson seemed at a loss as to how to out-psych him as he had so many other pretenders; Wenger appeared to visibly shrink from the battle, while Liverpool's new manager Rafa Benitez, initially at least, just looked confused. Even when the controversy over Mourinho's allegations that Barcelona manager Frank Rijkaard pressured the referee during the first leg of the Champions' League last sixteen match, or his finger to the lips gesture to Liverpool fans in the Carling Cup final, threatened to turn people against him, he always managed to turn things around. He trod a very fine line, but managed to keep everyone – players, fans and supporters – onside.

In the course of researching this book, I was staggered by the amount of times that a Mourinho quote beat many from the world of showbiz or politics to the accolade of quote of the week – staggered but not really surprised. Even after a dull nil–nil draw, Mourinho can always summon up something that people want to hear, some snippet that football fans will relay to each other the next day. The fans – and not only of Chelsea – see something of themselves in him, his intolerance of sloppy unmotivated players, his passion for his squad and his all-consuming desire to win, win, win. This is one of his abundant gifts, and one that Chelsea and the Premiership – if not Wenger and Ferguson – hope will grace the league for many years to come.

B. C.:
Life Before Chelsea

Everyone knew he was coming to Chelsea, but it was still an extraordinary sight. José Mourinho – and his team Porto – had won the Champions' League yet he seemed curiously emotionless. The man who had locked horns with Sir Alex Ferguson, upset Celtic fans and shepherded an unfancied team to two European trophies in as many years seemed like he was elsewhere, his mind perhaps drifting off towards London. Just a month later he was there, giving a press conference that announced the arrival of someone the Premiership would immediately take to their hearts. It was a meteoric rise by any standards – he'd only been a manager for just over four years before joining Chelsea – and now, at Stamford Bridge, Mourinho was there to show that his success with Porto had been no fluke.

Mourinho, unlike many managers, was never much of a footballer. He did play a handful of games for Rio Ave, a small Portuguese club, but realised that he would never make it as a top-class footballer. Instead he focused on studying and coaching, eventually taking his place as a university student to read sports science.

Mourinho had been an assistant coach for just over a year before becoming 'The Translator' for Bobby Robson at Sporting Lisbon in 1992. Despite his tender age in management terms – he was barely 30 – it was the start of a five year association with Robson, which would take him to Porto and Barcelona and eventually give him his big break. Under the tutelage of Robson – and later Louis Van Gaal – Mourinho learned his trade and honed his sharp managerial instincts, showing signs that he was becoming a top manager in his own right. It seemed only a matter of time before someone would make him an offer he couldn't refuse.

Benfica did just that, taking him on as head coach not long after the start of the 2000–1 season. But Mourinho's first taste of being in charge was not to be a happy one. After just nine games, of which Benfica won five, José was on his way – though whether he was pushed out or left of his own accord is something of a moot point. Either way, Benfica were left to rue the decision as Mourinho took the reigns at Super Liga minnows Uniao de Leina, leading them to the dizzy heights of fourth position. Mourinho was once again attracting attention and in 2001 was enticed back to Porto to save their faltering season. With a dazzling fifteen game run, in which they lost only twice, Mourinho guided Porto to third place in the Super Liga and the promise of a much improved campaign next time around.

The Porto side Mourinho inherited were talented yet disorganised, but Mourinho soon moulded them into champions. In the following two seasons they won back to back Super Liga titles, a pair of domestic cups, the UEFA cup and – of course – the Champions' League. It was an astonishing achievement, one that defied the expectations of even the most devoted of fans. The question was, could he replicate this success at Chelsea?

'Martin O'Neill is clever but I'm not stupid. I know what he's trying to do and it won't work. It's a European final and there are no favourites.'

Mourinho refuses to take the line that Celtic are underdogs before the 2003 UEFA Cup final.

'They'll have to adapt to us. We have more ball possession, more technical quality and more initiative than Celtic. If things go the way I hope we will face the Champions' League winners in the European Super Cup in Monaco.'

Super-confident ahead of the final in 2003.

'We don't know how to play defensively. My players would turn on me if I gave them such orders. Porto have been educated to try and win every game. From what I know Celtic also play only to win. I envisage a fantastic game with lots of goals . . . Whatever the result I've no doubts it will be a friendly final. The Scottish supporters drink more beer than the Portuguese but it will be a fantastic atmosphere.'

Mourinho anticipates an exciting – if boozy – atmosphere.

'It is our duty to Scotland and Portugal to put on such a beautiful game of football people will remember it for years and years. What have we got to lose? At the beginning of the season if you asked Celtic supporters and asked Porto supporters if they thought they would reach the final of a European competition, maybe 10 per cent would say yes. So we have produced a surprise for everybody and now we are both really on a high.'

Mourinho outlines the responsibilities of Celtic and Porto for their own leagues' reputation.

'I spoke to Bobby Robson last week, although not about this game. He always taught me to respect other people in football. He's a British man, but, because of me, I think he wants Porto to win on Wednesday.'

Mourinho enlists the help of his old boss before the Celtic v. Porto UEFA Cup final, 2003.

'The playing field and the climate is the same for both teams, so we can't use that to our benefit. But football at the highest level must be played on a better field than the one there tomorrow night. I am very sorry, but I have to be critical and say that the pitch is not good. You must be fair ... When you play in a UEFA Cup Final in May then it is difficult to accept that the pitch is not great. We are used to playing on a great surface – not on a brown surface.'

Mourinho blasts the pitch in Seville before the UEFA Cup final.

'I can't take any risks with him [star striker Derlei Silva]. If I could, I would put him in a glass dome to make sure he gets there in one piece.'

A novel new method of transportation is suggested before the UEFA Cup final.

'There will be no surprises for either team. Martin O'Neill is a good coach, and I think I am a good coach, and good coaches don't wake up on the wrong side of the bed and suddenly decide to do things they have never done before. I think both teams know the other pretty well.'

Mourinho seems well versed in what to expect from Celtic.

'Was the behaviour of Celtic's players normal in your country?'

It seems that José didn't quite expect Celtic to be *that* physical in the final.

'There was a lot of commitment in Celtic's game – commitment, toughness and aggression. I'm tempted to use another word, but I won't.'

Mourinho fights fire with fire after Porto angered Martin O'Neill with what he saw as time-wasting during the 2003 UEFA Cup final.

'Celtic use an aggressive style of play in the hope their opponents will buckle. But football will always be the winner and we showed that in Seville. We kept the ball and Celtic just ran all over the pitch trying to get to us with their horrible and aggressive style.'

José wades in to back Barcelona's criticisms of Celtic during their 2004–5 UEFA Cup campaign.

'I think in the whole game there was about 45 minutes of football . . . If an opponent comes to play like that and a referee gives them permission for this type of football, it is difficult.'

Mourinho was similarly unimpressed by Deportivo La Coruna's physical tactics in the semi-final of the 2004 Champions' League.

'We were the team with more quality and we did more to win the game. We gave a great example to the world that football is a festival. We put together a team of almost unknowns, players who don't earn millions but are rich in titles and quality. We're to be congratulated.'

A delighted Mourinho after winning his first European Trophy.

'I'm definitely staying on at Porto next season but I would like to move abroad in the future. I don't need to run away from this sort of success. I'm really looking forward to being in the Champions' League and it's the key to keeping some of the players as well. I don't think we can win it, though. Only the big sharks of European football, the ones who can afford to pay 20 or 30 million euros for a player, can win it. We're not in a position to do that.'

Ruling out the possibility of moving – Spurs were interested at the time – and winning the Champions' League.

'I think Chelsea is a complicated club because there is a lot of money but an enormous pressure to win something soon. I think the money will stop entering the club if they fail to win anything. Do you think it's bearable to keep this crazy investment and not to win something? I think not. I think the money will stop entering the club if they fail to win anything.'

Mourinho has his doubts about his future employers.

'There is a lot of emotion and sadness from a coach if his team has lost. I will shake his hand at Old Trafford . . . I understand he was a bit emotional because top players in his team should play better. He has seen his side dominated by a team with only 10 per cent of his budget.'

The start of the public 'discussions' with Sir Alex Ferguson after Porto had beaten United 2–1 in the first leg of their Champions' League match, October 2004.

'I think they are worried about us. They have 65,000 people behind them and a very powerful team. They have everything. So why are they afraid? I don't need to say stupid things or speak about cheating, or falling down, or referees. I speak only about football.'

Ahead of the second leg of the Champions' League last sixteen match with Manchester United, Mourinho cranks up the mind-games with Sir Alex, October 2004.

'The United coach said a player on the Porto team was a cheat and he simulated a foul. But I told him you should first look at the TV before you comment. If he is right, and Roy Keane didn't touch our goalkeeper Vitor Baia, I will apologise. But when he sees the replay and finds our player did not cheat, I want him to apologise. What he said is not right and you can't say these things without considering what you're saying.'

Mourinho after being asked by Sir Alex for an apology for the previous quote, asks for one himself.

'I don't hold any hope that Ferguson will call me to apologise. Ferguson did not call and I am not expecting him to call me. He has a bad attitude based on poor vision.'

Mourinho refuses to wait for his phone to ring.

'Sir Alex said congratulations at the end and we shook hands. That's what I like in football. Sometimes somebody is incorrect, I have done it before and I will do it again, and sometimes you play with words and try and put some pressure on the opposition but when the last whistle goes it's finished, you shake hands and I am happy with that.'

The end of the war of words between Ferguson and Mourinho. At least until the following season . . .

'I will go to Stamford Bridge as an enemy. I don't think enemies are welcome but I've got a ticket — and a bodyguard. I will go there because I'm a professional and what I want most now is to win the final. I don't feel any pressure at the moment because I don't talk with clubs, directors, presidents or owners. I'm very focused on my work.'

Mourinho – who was now odds on favourite to take over at Chelsea – talks security before watching the Chelsea v. Monaco Champions' League semi-final.

'Unforgettable. But let no one say unrepeatable.'

On winning the treble with Porto.

The Special One:
Mourinho on Himself

For someone who hogs the limelight even in the close
season, very little is known about José Mourinho aside
from what he has said publicly. Only one biography has
been published thus far (though two are forthcoming at
the time of writing) and that was principally about his
time at Porto. He is reluctant to talk of his early years,
and his life and opinions away from football are rarely
discussed. Though upfront and candid about his players,
other managers and all things football related, Mourinho is
intensely private about all other matters.

José Mario dos Santos Mourinho Felix, the son of
Portuguese goalkeeper Felix Mourinho, was born in 1963
in Setubal. He grew up in a mansion inherited from his
mother's uncle and inevitably fell in love with football.
Mourinho claims that he knew at a very young age that he
would not make the top-flight as a player and so
concentrated on coaching. His mother, Maria Julia,
enrolled him in business school when it became apparent
to her that football would not make Mourinho's fortune,
but he quit and set off to prove her wrong . . .

It's at this point that the Mourinho we are acquainted
with begins. What the following quotes show is how little
he is prepared to give away, almost as though every
interview or press call is an elaborate poker match. This
of course makes him difficult for everyone to read:
players, managers, fans alike, and also makes him all the

more fascinating. There is little mystery about most managers; they wear their hearts on their sleeves and make you feel as though you know them. Very few people outside of his clubs and his family would feel like they know Mourinho. Is he really that arrogant, or is that just part of the psychological aspect of the game? Is he really as strict as he makes out, or is there a softer, more gentle side to him?

These quotes don't seem to answer these questions, in fact they seem to pose more. But that is part of Mourinho's charm and these tantalising glimpses into the psyche only serve to heighten his mysterious charms.

'I'm not one who comes straight out of a bottle – I'm a special one . . . Obviously, if I don't reach my goals perhaps I will have to go home. But I don't think this will happen. I think at the end of my contract Chelsea will be interested in giving me a new one.'

José creates a nickname for himself in record time during his first press conference as Chelsea manager, June 2004.

'Everybody has his opinion and can write and say what they want or feel. I was taught to respect other opinions but at the same time my personality is not open to be influenced by critics or by opinions.'

Pre-season comments, August 2004.

'When you have a father, ex-top player, and your dream is to be like him but you feel you couldn't do it, your motivation comes from that point. I want to be really big in football. I feel I have some conditions to be a coach and manager. I start doing. I start loving it. I go to university and study sports science. This is a real passion and methodology.'

Explaining the roots behind the special one . . .

'If they don't touch me, I won't touch anyone. If they touch me, I'll be ready to hit back even harder.'

José issues a warning to his rivals and critics.

'I think I'm lucky because I'm coming to England as a European champion and I can imagine what it would be like if I came here on an ordinary CV. I want to say one thing: I didn't ask to come here. I was in a small country, beautiful in fact, trying to improve, and I became a European champion. Some English clubs came after me. I didn't go to church and pray "please take me to England". I don't pay to be here. Somebody trusted me and brought me here and I'm really happy about that because my family love it here and there is no worry. Yet some people always want to criticise, some people who hide behind their status of ex-players. Yet I am a European champion and, as that, I think I deserve a little respect.'

Mourinho rounds on his critics – and not for the last time – after beating Birmingham 1–0.

'Some people love me, some people don't love me so much. That's football, that's life.'

José reacts to being spat at by a Porto fan.

'I don't have to be jealous of Barcelona because they have 100 years of history and have won the European Cup once. I have only been managing for five years and I have the same amount of Champions' League trophies to my name.'

Mourinho talks himself up as bigger than Barcelona before their Champions' League match.

'I have had twenty years of honeymoons with my wife. The day that this club is not happy with me is the day that I go. At the moment, I'm very happy here and do not want to say goodbye. But when the club are not happy with me, or I am not happy with them, then it is the time to go.'

On being asked if his Chelsea honeymoon was over after defeats by Newcastle and Barcelona in February 2005.

'Do not tell me your movie. I am in a movie of my own.'

A cryptic response to some journalists' predictions of an Arsenal or Manchester United resurgence to knock Chelsea from the top of the Premiership.

'I have a good car, but only one at a time. I like good holidays with my family, I like us to live in a nice place, but as a football man the most important thing is to be working with the right people and with the right approach to things.'

Mourinho's simple pleasures.

'Truth is like olive oil, but the reality is that it sometimes appears too late ... I don't want to say anything except that oil always surfaces.'

In a comment reminiscent of a certain kung fu-fighting Frenchman, José responds to his touchline ban by UEFA.

'We have to fight the use of drugs because we want the truth. True managers, clean players and good referees. We want it really clean. We have a responsibility to try to help and control this situation. When people think that top sports people are involved with social drugs, it sends a bad message to the world and our kids. I am always a defender of control and punishment.'

Mourinho looks to clean up the game in the wake of drug scandals in football.

'I prefer four, three, three.'

His response to being asked if he was politically right or left wing in Tel Aviv.

'In Europe there is a boy daring to think high. He was ambitious, wanting to be informed, courageous in his entry into a world dominated by people united by links and conservative principles. It was domineering like an iceberg in which the mass of what we see at the surface makes us think there is nothing below it. The kid arrived, said he wanted to win and won. He said he was one of the best and he proved it. He said he did not want to be an integral part of the plan and remained independent. He said the sharks around him did not frighten him and he swam between them ... The moral of the story is not to listen to those who tell you not to play the violin but stick to the tambourine.'

The Special One talks about being The Special One.

'For sure I am. You want to try and succeed in your job like I have done in mine inside three years? You have no chance.'

A typically bullish response to being asked if he was still The Special One.

'I have loved football since I can remember and I understand the evolution of football and the modern needs of football.'

Expressing his devotion in his first press conference as Chelsea manager.

'The English Premiership is recognised as the best league in the world and I am really excited at the prospect of competing week in, week out at the highest level in England as well as in Europe. I have been asked how I will cope with the pressure, how I will cope with these players, how I will cope with the urgent ambition to win titles. You don't have to ask me again because that's what I live for.'

Another statement of intent in June 2004.

'I think you have to act a little bit and to show sometimes a different face. I am not bad at it. I'm not the "special one". I was under pressure when I arrived as a European champion and I thought I wasn't respected. The press put 50 difficult questions to me — can you succeed, are you ready for this and are you ready for that? I said, "what you want is this — I'm the special one", and you never forget it.'

Talking to Gary Lineker about those pre-season comments.

'I put myself in the firing line straight away by saying things that some people understand and some don't, Like, for example, "I'm special", "I want to win in the first season", "I don't care about the power of Manchester United and Arsenal", and "I don't care that no one in English football was champion in the first season", I might have put myself in the spotlight but, at the same time, I woke up my people and I also put them under a little bit of pressure. I said: "All of you are top players, but nobody won a Premiership or a Champions' League, and you are not successful players until you win." So I made them think. I hurt them a bit but I created a big ambition in the team. It was risky but it worked.'

Mourinho's media tactics explained in full.

'I chose between England, Italy and Spain and think I made the right choice as I enjoy it here so much. The thing I don't enjoy is the way the media talk about us. I feel as if the knives are being aimed in our direction while the flowers are in another.'

England is something of a double-edged sword for Mourinho.

'If I want to have an easy job, working with the big protection of what I have already done before, I would stay at Porto. Beautiful blue chair, UEFA Champions, God, and after God, me.'

Another classic quote that had the assorted journalists scurrying to their editors . . .

'I don't have much of a social life because I don't have much time for one but my family have settled down, they are happy, they are adapting and when they are happy it's easier for me. In relation to my job at Chelsea and the way I'm spending my time every day, I'm really happy because I'm doing what I love to do.'

Mourinho in September 2004.

At Home:
The Premiership 2004–5

At the end of the 2003–4 season Chelsea's trophy cabinet was bare. Despite finishing second to the unbeaten Arsenal in the Premiership, and coming agonisingly close to the Champions' League final, it became immediately apparent that the 'Tinker Man' Claudio Ranieri was not going to be the man to bring silverware to Stamford Bridge. Even as the season was drawing to a close, names were being bandied about as to who would take over (Mr Eriksson's most prominently of all). But by the time Mourinho had lifted the Champions' League trophy with Porto it was clear, despite strong links with Liverpool, that he would be on his way to Chelsea. What he achieved in that first season is nothing short of remarkable.

Joining in June 2004, Mourinho immediately made an impact, both in his appearance and approach. Here was a man who looked, sounded and acted in a cultured, almost nonchalant manner, but had already set in motion a physically gruelling pre-season training plan and warned players that they would have to prove their motivation to him. Before a ball had even been kicked, Mourinho had set out his stall: they were going to win games, even if they had to grind out every game 1–0.

If Mourinho needed a statement of intent he got it in the first game, beating Manchester United by that exact scoreline: one that would be repeated several times over before Christmas. Their stinginess in defence became both a mark of pride for Mourinho, and a stick with which his critics would beat him. He and his team were accused of being boring, unadventurous, lacking the excitement that people demanded. Of course, Mourinho was still good value after the game, but the lack of goals was a concern. This was compounded by back to back nil-nil draws, two narrow victories, then their first defeat, in October, away at Manchester City.

This unexpected loss, however, galvanised the team and their manager. They hit four in their next two games, then beat a resolute Everton team by a single goal, before hammering local rivals Fulham 4–1. The season had truly begun. Soon four goals in a game was a regular occurrence. They beat Manchester United 3–1 at the Theatre of Dreams. John Terry and Frank Lampard were acclaimed as players of the season, Joe Cole had forced himself into the England team after learning so much from Mourinho, and of course they won the Carling Cup.

Manchester City were the only team to beat Mourinho's men on the way to a Premiership record of 95 points with only fifteen goals conceded in their 38 games. To achieve this in any season is incredible; to manage it in your first, with a brand new squad, is practically unheard of. In just one season Mourinho proved beyond doubt that there is something very special about him.

'Liverpool are a team that interests everyone. Chelsea does not interest me so much because it is a new project with lots of money invested in it. I think it is a project which, if the club fail to win everything, then Abramovich could retire and take the money out of the club. It is interesting for a coach to have the money to hire quality players, but you never know if a project like this will bring success.'

Proof that Mourinho does change his mind occasionally – it took him two months to decide to take on the 'project'.

'Chelsea last won the title 50 years ago so I knew they needed to win things. But under Mr Ranieri they could win nothing.'

José fires a broadside against his predecessor.

'We have top players and, sorry if I'm arrogant, we have a top manager.'

José Mourinho introduces himself to the British press in his own inimitable style.

'They do not have to run one single lap and yet they are more tired at the end of the session than they were in the past. Every day I prepare the exercises, the time for the exercises, the time for rest between repetitions, the time between exercises, the finish time when I give the fitness guys time to relax them and stretch them before they go home or come to lunch. I think they are starting to understand how specific the training is. Good players adapt easily.'

Mourinho outlines his terrifying training schedule.

'I want a small club, 21 players plus the goalkeepers and no more. I hate to work with big squads.'

Mourinho immediately spelling out that certain players would be on the way out very soon . . .

'Motivation is the most important thing. Some of them can and they don't want, some of them want and they can't. We want players who can do it and at the same time want to do it. When you look now at Chelsea players' CVs it's similar to Porto's players' before I arrived. Nobody won important things. You have two European champions here, Claude Makelele and Paulo Ferreira. But nobody won the Premiership. No one has the taste of big victories.'

Spelling out what he needs from his players, August 2004.

'When I met Mr Abramovich he never once demanded we win the Premiership. I just feel we can do it. I'm at a club that wants to win. I understand people saying he has bought the title by spending millions but it doesn't concern me. After him there are lots of people, everyone plays their part. If we win anything, then it will be together, not as individuals.'

Deflecting criticism of the Abramovich billions . . .

'I don't have to control Mr Abramovich. He has to control me.'

And reminding him who's boss . . .

'Nobody in the club can tell me to buy a player. But they can say to me, you don't buy the player you want.'

And again . . .

'We deserved the victory but they didn't deserve the defeat.'

Magnanimous in victory against Manchester United on the first day of the season – Sir Alex must have been surprised.

'I am really pleased with the spirit of my team. They played when they had to play and fought when they had to fight. They adapted to the style of play of their opponents. For me as a coach I am really pleased when I see strikers defending as well as mine did. You don't start building a house with the roof.'

After their second 1–0 win of the season against Birmingham.

'The atmosphere in the dressing-room afterwards is what I want to see. I don't want them just happy when they beat Manchester United but not so happy when they beat Everton. Every game has to be a final. If you want to be champions, every game is a final. The players are definitely getting that mentality and taking it into every match. They give everything on the pitch and leave every bit of themselves out there. Everybody knew how important it was to win this game. And in the last period of the game they understood that the match could have turned the other way when we were under pressure. But we changed the organisation so well that we could have played however long it took and still kept a clean sheet. They get over all the walls that the opponent puts in front of them. For me that is a fantastic mentality to see in your players.'

A motivational and praising post-match comment after yet another 1–0 win, this time against Everton.

'I must admit that if Roman Abramovich helped me out in training we would be bottom of the league. And if I had to work in his world of big business we would be bankrupt.'

José makes it quite clear *again* who runs the footballing side of Chelsea.

'I believe in home players and Peter Kenyon and Roman Abramovich think the same. Especially as a foreign manager, I feel a bit responsible for the English national team and English players ... Supporters fall in love with players that they feel have the same feeling for the club. You don't need to be made at the club to do that – I don't think the Chelsea supporters have any doubt that Claude Makelele very much wants Chelsea to succeed – but it does help.'

Mourinho explains the importance of home talent, February 2005.

'If you give me four years I promise we will win the title. In certain matches you will defend in the last fifteen minutes. Some people may not be happy but a few days later they will see we have three more points. If Mr Abramovich likes 5–4, I am sure he hates 4–5. So if you have to choose between 4–5 and 1–0, you have to go for the 1–0.'

For the early part of the season at least, Chelsea certainly went for 1–0 . . .

'I have been a champion before and I know what to do. At the moment we have six points and are top of the league after two very difficult games. You can say what you want but we will keep going our way.'

Responding to yet more criticism of his team's lack of goals.

'We shouldn't wait for flowers to come from people. Maybe we will get some at the end of the season but right now it's very difficult.'

Thinking about the Premiership crown already, September 2004.

'One of my assistants said that on the last day of the season the Kings Road will be crazy. But I said that maybe we can win it one or two weeks before the end of the season.'

A confident Mourinho, a full six months before the end of the Premiership season.

'We can win four, we can lose four, but the way we play suggests we have to win something. But if you give me the Premiership today, I'd be happy.'

In February Mourinho pondered the possibility of a unique quadruple come the end of the season.

'We are on top at the moment, but not because of the club's financial power. We are in contention for a lot of trophies because of my hard work, coaching sessions and the team ethic I have instilled here. My philosophy is that you don't win a game during the 90 minutes. A winning team is made day by day, training session by training session, minute by minute.'

Mourinho takes a very personal view of how successful Chelsea are ahead of the Carling Cup final.

'They didn't play football, they just defended, defended, defended. They may as well have parked the team bus in front of their goal.'

Mourinho was not impressed at all after drawing with Spurs.

'Bolton made life very difficult for us and I prefer to give them credit. What can we do? Shoot the ball out of the air? It's a very difficult style of football and there's nothing you can do.'

José proposes a novel way to deal with an aerial threat . . .

'There must be a microclimate here. It hadn't even rained and yet the pitch was like a swimming pool.'

Blackburn's Ewood Park and its magical meteorology.

'Blackburn tried to foul us and foul us and foul us. They felt they couldn't beat us playing football so they tried to beat us in a different way. They were direct, aggressive, nasty and intimidating.'

It wasn't just the weather that upset José in Blackburn . . .

'We will invest a lot in the scouting department. We want to have the best possible network of scouts around the world and to produce our own players because when we are at this level we can only buy the best players in the world.'

On the importance of the academy, May 2005.

'Where are the best players? At the best clubs in the world – and they don't want to sell. So you want to improve your team and it is difficult. Even with money you cannot buy them so you have to produce. We know it takes time but my contract is for five years and I hope in five years that the Chelsea production line is better than it is now.'

Mourinho seems a little frustrated in his recent transfer dealings, May 2005.

'It's not easy at this minute. Teams don't want to sell players and players are afraid to come to Chelsea because they won't be first choice.'

Proving that the transfer market has always been tough for him, José laments not being able to sign a defender before the 2004–5 season starts.

'Youth development is crucial. We must have a nucleus of strong personalities, and if possible with people with the culture of the club. Would I like to have a heart of Chelsea boys made here? Yes I would.'

Mourinho dreams of a squad of Lampards and Terrys, June 2005.

'My heart is with Chelsea and the fantastic group of players I have, but the vision of the owner and the board for the future of Chelsea is also one I want to be part of. I am totally behind this project and their support in achieving it means Chelsea is the place where I will be happiest in my work.'

All is rosy after signing a new contract . . .

'It was a moment of frustration, impotence and injustice. I felt a lack of enchantment and was thinking that Chelsea were not defending me in the way I thought was ideal. But I am where I want to be and where I believe I will be for the next five years. I sincerely believe that.'

Though it wasn't all plain sailing . . .

'With the team we put out we showed we have other trophies ahead of the FA Cup but we came to win so we're not happy. But it's not a drama, we're in a fantastic position to win the league . . . there are many reasons to forget this game and move on.'

After a rare defeat, on this occasion in the FA Cup at the hands of Newcastle.

'When you're fighting to be champions you need to fight with your sleeves up to get points. We try to play good football and score goals. I can understand the supporters want to see Damien Duff and Arjen Robben on the pitch and scoring goals. We won 1–0 in a difficult situation, playing with heart and taking the points. Everyone speaks about the goals but there are also the clean sheets.'

Singing the praises of his defence after beating Aston Villa on Boxing Day, 2004.

'There is so much ground for the teams chasing us to make up. If it goes from ten to twelve or thirteen points then maybe it will be over. Could you ever imagine that with all the new players and a new coach we could be ten clear at this stage? Of course ten points is ten points, it is better than seven and it is better than five.'

A maths class from Mourinho, January 2005.

'We won because of our fantastic defensive organisation and because of a fantastic defensive performance by the team – and some individuals. The way both teams fought and tried to win the game means I think a draw would be a fair result. But at the right moment we had that little bit of luck that champions need to have in crucial moments.'

After beating Liverpool 1–0 in January 2005.

'Arsenal have a great group of players in their first team, but after that they have young people. Talented but very young. Only Manchester United have a squad like ours, two mature players for every position.'

Mourinho criticises Wenger's youthful side, December 2004.

'It can be correct that we will lose a lot of points in the north of the country. We don't know. But, for sure, Manchester United lose points in the south. They lost three points at Stamford Bridge, they lost three points at Portsmouth and they lost two points at Fulham. So, for sure, they have a problem in the south. Maybe I will face something that I don't know, that is unbelievable, up north. I look forward to it.'

Mourinho relishes the challenge laid down by Sir Alex in December 2004.

'He is so much in love with the club. He's not a person to sell the club in a few years and go away. He's completely committed and that's good.'

A little bit of kissing up to Roman Abramovich, May 2005.

'I believe in my team and in my club. We are a family, that is why you could see everybody from Chelsea hugging when we won the Carling Cup. I am not interested in managing England. First, I think the team is in good hands and second, when Sven Goran Eriksson leaves, I believe it should go back to an Englishman.'

Mourinho rules out becoming England's Special One.

'Listen, give me the shirt and give Steve Clarke the shirt and we'll go out and work harder than you lot have done.'

From an inspired team-talk against Bolton to clinch the title.

'It is perfect. The record was our motivation. We wanted to beat it and this is a special moment. It is the perfect way to do it, at a great stadium against a team who in Sir Alex Ferguson have a manager who leads by example in success and fair play.'

Sir Alex was undoubtedly overjoyed to be complimented in such a way after being beaten 3–1 in his own back yard, making sure that Chelsea beat the Premiership points record that United set . . .

'To win the Premiership and prove we are the best makes me very happy. We are a young group who have worked together just this season.'

It makes him happy, but not happy enough . . .

'I now know that a lot of people didn't think we could do it in our first season but we did. My nature is not to be happy with what we have done. We want more. I've got my hands on the trophy but now I want to win it again. This is the start of a process not the end. I want more for me and Chelsea.'

Mourinho looks forward to bringing the cup back to Stamford Bridge in 2006.

'I am not concerned about how Chelsea are viewed morally. What does concern me is that we are treated in a different way to other clubs. Some clubs are treated as devils, some are treated as angels. I don't think we are so ugly that we should be seen as the devil and I don't think Arsène Wenger and David Dein are so beautiful that they should be viewed as angels.'

Mourinho begins the season in typical fashion, July 2005.

'I saw the Manchester United players and manager go for a lap of honour after losing to us in their last home game. In Portugal if you do this they throw bottles at you.'

Dishing it out to Manchester United and Sir Alex, July 2005.

'When we played against West Brom on 30 October, Arsenal drew at home and we went top for the first time. After that we never left that position and you increasingly feel you are strong, tactically and mentally. But for me the moment when we celebrated for the first time was after we beat Tottenham. We were on the bus on the way back and Arsenal lost at Bolton. Our lead went from five points to eight points. It was the first time we had celebrated. Now I am happy, tired and I would like to go on holiday.'

Mission accomplished, May 2005.

Playing Away:
The Champions' League 2004–5

It was difficult not to know that Mourinho arrived at
Chelsea as European Champion – he for one would not
let people forget it – but with this fact came expectation.
Porto's 2004 win was an unlikely victory, but there was no
pressure to win the competition. With the chairman's
seemingly limitless funds, the exact opposite would be the
case. The Premiership would be the priority, but . . .

Chelsea's previous season's Champions' League run was
exciting, but ultimately fruitless. The confusing – some
might say baffling – substitutions of Claudio Ranieri meant
that Chelsea crashed out to Monaco in the semi-finals.
The aggregate score was 5–3. In the other semi-final,
Porto v. Deportivo, the aggregate was just 1–0, somewhat
typifying the difference in styles between the two
managers . . .

After two successful European campaigns, it was clear that
Mourinho wanted to – and believed he could – make it
three successful campaigns in a row. The initial round also
threw up an added incentive: Chelsea would meet Porto
in Group H.

Chelsea won their first four games at a canter – including
a victory over Mourinho's old club – and were assured of
passage into the knockout stages. Mourinho, however, was
both praising and critical of his team. Some of the finest
football his team had put together so far saw them easily

beat Paris Saint Germain, CSKA and Porto at home, but they lost their final game to his former club in Portugal. Mourinho was not happy at the result, and the thought of facing another old club – Barcelona – in the next round wasn't much of a consolation.

As it turned out, the next two rounds were quite unlike anything Mourinho could have envisaged. It was his allegations that Anders Frisk and Barcelona's Frank Rijkaard had spoken at half time in the first leg that really changed the complexion of the campaign. His comments earned him a ban from attending the next two games, and jeopardised the campaign. It seemed he had gone too far this time.

But as goals flew in from all over the place against Barcelona, and in the following round against Bayern Munich, the controversy appeared to have waned slightly. In four massively entertaining – and nerve wracking – games, Mourinho's men overcame two of the finest sides in Europe to set up an all English semi-final with Liverpool.

Having beaten Liverpool three times already that season, and being 30-odd points ahead of them in the Premiership, Chelsea were the overwhelming favourites. They remained so despite a nil-nil draw at Stamford Bridge, where several chances went begging. The mood of the players, and of Mourinho was buoyant.

One solitary – and highly contentious – goal changed all that.

In front of a jubilant Anfield, all still relishing revenge after Mourinho's finger-to-lip gesture at the Carling Cup final, Chelsea's Champions' League dream was over.

Mourinho was understandably tetchy after the game – and made his annoyance quite clear. To him, he had been wrongfully denied a trophy he regards as his own. Very few people would bet against him lifting it again.

'The team played the perfect game. I was pleased with the result, pleased with the performance and pleased with every single player. I think we played top-class football and controlled the game from the first minute until the last. Defensively we were incredible. At the end of the day, the game looked easy. But it was my players who made it look easy.'

After beating Paris St-Germain 3–0 in the group stages of the 2004–5 Champions' League.

'There are a lot of players at Porto who are my players, but there are no friends during 90 minutes.'

José warns his former club before the Champions' League group game against Porto.

'We lost at Manchester City and your life changes when you lose. But they showed a good reaction and the happiness is back. We played great matches against Porto and Paris St Germain. This wasn't great but we were strong mentally.'

After beating CSKA Moscow 2–0, October 2004.

'Petr Cech, John Terry and Ricardo Carvalho were absolutely amazing. It's a magic triangle and all the other players were fitting in. We have been fantastic in all four matches and this was the most difficult one because CSKA played great too.'

After beating CSKA 1–0 away in the Champions' League group stages.

'A guy said to me "We're not going to do anything now because you have this final but after, you're a dead man. As soon as you get back to Porto, your bed is made, we're going to get you, you don't have a chance."'

Mourinho recounts the chilling threats he received before the Chelsea v. Porto Champions' League match.

'Frank Rijkaard's history as a player can't be compared with my history, as his is fantastic and mine is zero. As a manager though, my history cannot be compared to his. He has zero titles and I have a lot of them.'

José plays some mind-games with the Barcelona coach before their last sixteen clash.

'I love Barcelona and I know that the people love me. In the club I have in every corner a friend so it will be very, very, very emotional for me to go there.'

On returning to Barcelona – where he was assistant coach – in the last sixteen of the Champions' League.

'I am very happy. Since I left Barcelona in 2000, I haven't been back. I left as assistant and I go back as European champion and Chelsea boss so it is fantastic for me. As a football team they are not better than us. Nobody is the underdog. It's 50-50 or maybe 51-49 to us.'

Confident ahead of the Barcelona clash.

'I am very happy I have a fantastic group, this is a fantastic club, with a fantastic project and we are going in the right direction. This season is better than anyone could have dreamed of, even me.'

Before quarter-final of the Champions' League against Bayern Munich.

'In the first leg I never feel the pressure of having to win or not concede because we are at home. Nor is there pressure to score or draw just because you are playing away. I hate this kind of mentality. I've told the players already that I don't want it.'

Laying down his tactics before playing Bayern Munich.

'I have to make decisions, not emotionally, but just to try to get the best from my team. There's no panic. We must not play the first game at home thinking that we have to win or that we have got to get a result to get to the final. If we don't win at home, we don't win. We can win the second game. So that is the most important factor. We must not panic for a result at home. You cannot be crazy and chase a result at home.'

The pressure mounts before the first leg of the semi-final against Liverpool in the Champions' League.

'Anfield is a beautiful atmosphere. In the Champions' League semi-finals, it will be even more beautiful.'

Mourinho in poetic mood before the semi-final second leg.

'In a Champions' League tie 0–0 at home is a good result. The result leaves me very, very, very confident we will get to the final. We will score goals in Liverpool and they will have to play a different way. 99.9 per cent of Liverpool fans will be thinking at the moment they have one foot in the final – but they aren't.'

Bold words from Mourinho, however . . .

'Liverpool scored, if you can say that they scored, because maybe you should say the linesman scored.'

Heartbreak after *that* goal.

'You should bring the linesman in here and ask why he gave the goal. To do that you have to be 100 per cent that the ball went in and my players say it was not. It was a goal that came from the moon – from the Anfield Road stands. I don't know from where . . . You can't tell from TV. Only one person has decided the future of a team. I make mistakes, my players make mistakes; he made a mistake. The best team lost.'

Mourinho's anger was barely contained . . .

'I felt the power of Anfield, it was magnificent. I felt it didn't interfere with my players but maybe it interfered with other people and maybe it interfered with the result . . . We are very sad, but you must understand what football is. They scored and we didn't so they go through.'

In a more reflective mood after the semi-final exit.

'The semi-final defeat to Monaco left them with a very bad feeling because they had everything in their hands. I could not fault the players at Liverpool. We were not at our maximum level at that time. No Duff or Robben, away from home and there were no other solutions to be more dangerous against a very defensive team. That will not happen again. It is never bad to reach the Champions' League semi-finals, because a lot of the big teams went out before then. We are talking about Arsenal, Manchester United, Inter Milan, Bayern, Barcelona and Real Madrid. It was disappointing, especially in the way we lost it. But when you cool down, go home, you realise what you did is normal and is not to be ashamed of.'

Upbeat about the disappointment of the Champions' League semi-final, July 2005.

'The Champions' League is a competition where only a great team can win, but only a great team with luck. In Premiership only a great team wins because it's 38 matches. It's not luck.'

Mourinho hopes for some good fortune in next season's Champions' League.

'If you ask me what we need to totally guarantee winning the Champions' League it is for goals against us to only be allowed when the ball is totally and 100 per cent over the line and in the goal.'

If anyone thought he was going to let the semi-final be forgotten, they were very wrong . . .

José's Way:
Mourinho's Philosophy of Football

Mourinho's philosophy of football is deceptively simple: do not concede goals. Indeed, in his first two months at Chelsea the amount of 1–0 victories had some people suggesting that he was overly defensive, too cautious for the Premiership. But, it now seems that there was far more going on in the mind of Mourinho than simply stifling the opposition and nicking the odd goal here or there. Winning was – and remains – the most important thing to him, but it slowly became apparent that he was reading the division and seeing how he could adapt the team and its tactics to dominate the division. At first he may have appeared cagey, but later on in the season the effect was explosive.

So what is it that marks Mourinho out as a different kind of manager? At first it's not easy to see. He is fanatical about teamwork, about all members of his squad being 100 per cent motivated for the cause. Extensive and intensive training is fundamental to his methodology as is a massive emphasis on preparation – perhaps a hangover from his days of writing scouting reports for both his father and Bobby Robson. Above all, he is a strict disciplinarian and is ruthless in his pursuit of victory. Names seem not to phase him; if a player is underperforming, no matter how much money he is worth, Mourinho will have no hesitation in dropping him. But none of these qualities are unique. Where he comes into his own is using all of the aforementioned attributes to make his teams believe that they will win, and that they are unbeatable.

Motivation is the key to much of Mourinho's success. Before Chelsea, his spending power was next to nothing and he could only rely on the players he had and those he could pick up cheaply. Of course, at Chelsea that has all changed, but the principle has remained the same. Joe Cole, for example, has learned from Mourinho and has developed beyond all recognition, a reminder of those more fiscally challenged days.

Mourinho's style is a wonderful amalgam of different influences: British passion, Continental tactics and a psychologist's eye for knowing how to build solid teams. Even though he has had the money at his disposal, Mourinho hasn't chased the big names simply for the sake of having them. Galactico culture does not fit with his philosophy, supposing as it does that the player is bigger than the club. Whether the club is the richest or poorest in the world, Mourinho shows that by reclaiming the basics – preparation, motivation, effort – you can succeed at any level.

'Football is a game based on emotion and intelligence. Anyone can be clever; the trick is not to think the other guy is stupid.'

In a philosophical mood after Porto's victory over Manchester United in the second leg of their Champions' League last sixteen match in 2004.

'From here each practice, each game, each minute of your social life must centre on the aim of being champions. First-teamer will not be a correct word. I need all of you. You need each other. We are a TEAM. 'Motivation + Ambition + Team + Spirit = SUCCESS.'

From a leaked letter to Chelsea players, Mourinho explains his key to winning trophies.

'My players are always the best players in the world, even if they aren't.'

That is unless you upset him . . .

'Don't tell me one week later that you don't like Harlington, don't like the weather, or the family is not happy in England. I don't want a player who is not totally committed to my methodology.'

A warning to the foreign contingent at Chelsea.

'In every family, sometimes you have problems, when you have ten, twenty, 30 people in a group working together, however good it is, there are always going to be problems.'

After rumours of players being unsettled at Stamford Bridge, Mourinho explains the difficulties of his second family.

'From what I can tell from a distance . . . Real Madrid are unbalanced. They have great figures and mediocre players. They are missing players of "medium quality". Those players that I call low-profile, that offend nobody.'

José turns on the Galactico culture of Real Madrid.

'5–4 is a hockey score, not a football score. I did not see the game but I can tell you now that the defenders were a disgrace. In training I often play matches of three against three and when the score reaches 5–4, I send the players back to the dressing-rooms because they are not defending properly. So to get a result like that in a game of eleven against eleven is disgraceful.'

Mourinho manages to put the backs up of both Spurs *and* Arsenal after their cricket-score Premiership match, November 2004.

'I cannot be pleased when my team loses. I am a professional and I want to win every game. Only stupid people don't understand that I want to win every game.'

Particularly when it's your old club: after Porto's 2–1 win over Chelsea in the Champions' League, December 2004.

'On Friday we practised defending, on Saturday we practised attacking. On Sunday we practised the transition from attack to defence. On Monday we practised the transition from defence to attack and on Tuesday we practised set-pieces.'

He makes it sound so simple . . . This was the training pattern before Porto's 2004 Champions' League final.

'Victories don't come from the moon. They come out of our hearts, out of our legs, out of our brains. The players are ready to do everything to get the results we need.'

Mourinho in determined mood, November 2004.

'We have had to play two matches in three days — which is foreign to many of them — and although I understand the traditions of football here at this time of year, it is not good for your health to do it. You can sit back and smoke cigars, one after another, and it is a good life, but it is not actually good for you.'

The fixture pile-up makes José come over all Cuban.

'Pressure is to be nine points behind. I don't feel pressure when I'm in front. When you are behind you need to get results and at the same time you need to wait for the people in front of you to lose matches. I prefer our position to being nine points behind.'

In response to comments made by Gary Neville and others that the pressure was all on Chelsea.

'All you need is a strong group of players – you don't need a Hollywood star. What the devil is a Galactico anyway? The image comes from the social lives, and fame the players have achieved. It is those Galacticos that I distrust.'

A derisory comment aimed towards the Galactico culture of Real Madrid – misconstrued to be directed towards David Beckham.

'Sometimes, you're proud when they win, sometimes when they lose. I was proud today.'

Chelsea's exit from the FA Cup in February 2005 was taken on the chin by Mourinho.

'[I aim] To give my best, to improve things and to create the football team in relation to my image and my football philosophy.'

A mission statement from The Special One, June 2004.

'I have read I have to prove a lot in English football. Sir Alex Ferguson is the only European champion in this country, nobody else, so I have to prove what?'

Bullish once more, in the face of criticism, March 2005.

'Being manager at Chelsea is like being a director general of a big company. What is the difference between managing Microsoft and managing John Terry and Frank Lampard?'

Mourinho give Bill Gates a run for his money . . .

'I can be in love with players for what they did this season but if they don't do it next season, I'm not in love anymore . . . It is all about internal competition. We will have the same group of players but with two or three new faces. It is important to create new motivations.'

José proves flighty in his affections.

'I was really surprised because in English football I wasn't expecting such etiquette. If an elbow situation happens in my country, Portugal, or in Italy, Spain or South America, then that is our culture. But you are, and you deserve to be, kings of fair play. That is why many people in the world are in love with your football.'

Robbie Savage's elbow on Mateja Kezman was something of a wake-up call to the physical nature of the Premiership. After beating Birmingham 1–0 away from home, August 2004.

'I always try to be direct with my men, but I cannot take the same approach with all of them, Some I speak to every day, others hardly at all. I don't like to give players hope when there are no chances for them.'

Mourinho's man management skills are rightly regarded as one of the best in the business, September 2004.

'I never speak about my players when they make big mistakes. I never consider one player individually guilty for a defeat, if anyone is guilty it's the manager.'

José takes responsibility for poor performances, November 2004.

'I don't like to play the 4-4-2 in two lines, I like the match in between the lines and players with dynamic creativity to do that.'

Mourinho sets out his tactical stall before the start of the 2004–5 season.

'I am curious about the kids who play street football. Sometimes it can be good to play without a coach. In the street you can play free football. You can find boys with quality. I need a special player. If he cannot say "I'm special" he cannot do it. You may call it arrogant but that's what I need.'

Mourinho outlines what he looks for in a young player, as plans for a 'Soccer Idol' television programme are revealed in May 2005.

'Unlike others, I don't consider stability in a squad as a crucial factor to whether a side is successful. A team has to be taught by the coach in the right way, be able to play in the manager's image and know their job well enough to do it with their eyes closed – and that isn't about having people working together for years. It's about the coach getting it right, hard work and taking good practice sessions.'

Mourinho gives some clues as to how he managed to transform Chelsea in just one year.

'As a manager, it is up to you to be able to make it work. You have to make the club knit together on all levels. If I instil this in my senior players, they can pass down their knowledge and spirit to all the newcomers. The players are my biggest allies and I don't forget that. I would almost say they are my on-field assistants. The secret isn't the length of time the players have worked with each other, it is that fact we all work together closely. And ambition is the weapon that makes you play well.'

Mourinho makes it clear how important he is to the team, May 2004.

'We went into the season wanting to win everything. You have to put players in the right frame of mind and convince them they can pull off any result. These days coaches must be psychologists.'

José shows how much there is to modern management.

'I want to know everything. I try to know everything about the players, I try to know the way the opposition's coach will be thinking, how he'll react at certain key moments.'

Knowledge is power at Stamford Bridge.

'The Italian league is the tactical league. The Spanish league is the technical league. The English league is about passion. When I thought I could have success here it is because I thought I could mix that English passion with tactical organisation and so our team became tactical. Boring for some, I don't know why, but tactical. To be fair, I think we are the best team in history because we beat the record.'

After winning the Premiership with 95 points – a new record.

The Players:
Mourinho on His Own and Others

While it's true that managers are nothing without their players, it seems likely that Mourinho would argue that players are nothing without their manager. The relationship he has with his own players is sometimes hard to understand. On the one hand he is a passionate defender of them, on the other a harsh taskmaster who will mete out criticism without holding back. There are times when he appears distant and aloof, other occasions where he almost looks like one of the squad. But whatever inconsistencies there are, it is immediately obvious that he sees his players as his most valuable commodity – not necessarily in personal terms, but in how they fit into his team.

Looking at the players he has bought, it's interesting that he has brought in few very big names. While Real Madrid went after Galacticos, Mourinho's Chelsea have tried to buy the best players for the system that the manager believes works best. Wayne Rooney, for example, would have been easily affordable yet, even after his barn-storming performances in Euro 2004, Mourinho didn't think he would bring something extra to his team. Shaun Wright-Phillips was bought to give Robben, Duff and Cole some cover, not simply to add a big name to the squad. This has meant that the majority of his signings have been successful – if a little pricy.

In the two pre-seasons that Mourinho has experienced at Chelsea, he has complained about the same thing: not being able to get the players he most wants. If the saga of Steven Gerrard's off/on transfer was enough to bear, the Michael Essien debacle of bid and counter-bid that dragged on before the 2005–6 season started, and the persistent rumours of a world record transfer fee for Andriy Shevchenko, have only compounded the problem. Mourinho's search for a top goal scorer has also floundered with Didier Drogba too inconsistent, considering the money paid for his services, Mateja Kezman proving to be a bitter disappointment and Hernan Crespo still seemingly unsettled in London. Money, it seems, can't always buy you what you want.

Mourinho is a winner and wants his players to behave in the same way as he does. By inspiring and motivating, and occasionally admonishing them, he has taken the Chelsea players by the scruff of their neck and turned them into worthy champions.

'He scores goals, a lot of goals. I like him because he is multi-functional; he adapts to different roles in the attacking position. He is not just the pure striker to play as a target man. He can play also with two strikers in the middle, as a winger from the right side. He is a complete, multi-functional player.'

Mourinho before signing Mateja Kezman . . .

'When a kid of eighteen plays like he did, it is amazing but we have other priorities.'

Mourinho deflects yet another rumour about trying to sign young master Rooney.

'Drogba is one of the best strikers in Europe and since I started talking to him I feel he needs a better club in a better league to show how good he is.'

£24-million-man Didier Drogba is perhaps still looking for that league . . .

'He is one of the best players in the world. He is the best in our squad. He is super-fast but when he gets into a passing or shooting position he normally chooses well.'

Mourinho on Arjen Robben – a judgement that holds a little better than his of Drogba and Kezman.

'I told Mutu, you are already a rich boy, you won a lot of money, you are still in a big contract. So no problem with your future about money, no problem about prestige in your home country. When you go back to Romania you will be one of the kings. But five years after you leave football nobody remembers you. Only if you do big things. This is what makes history.'

Adrian Mutu made a very different impression after joining Chelsea . . .

'His game has two faces – a beautiful one and one that I didn't like. He still has a lot to learn, a lot. After his goal, I needed eleven players to defend and I had just ten. He was not good enough for me.'

Joe Cole, who had just scored the winner against Liverpool, feels the wrath of Mourinho's obsession with clean sheets.

'We have had a conversation and I said: "No chance of leaving. Don't think about it because I need everybody." It's just a question of getting a chance. I've told him he's a good player, he works well and has a lot of ambition but at this moment the team is winning, playing very well and I'd be stupid to change it too much.'

A more positive report for Joe Cole from Mr Mourinho.

'Sudden mood swings, isolation within the group, unexpected injuries, fatigue, difficulty in concentrating, early morning escapes from traffic police, public statements which were untrue and made no sense – there were many situations which caused us to wonder.'

On Adrian Mutu. Enough said.

'John [Terry] would be worth a minimum of £50 million in the market, although of course he is not for sale. If every ten years we produce a John Terry then the work of the academy is done. It is better to produce quality than numbers.'

On the brilliant – and expensive – John Terry.

'When a club has John Terry, Ricardo Carvalho, William Gallas and Robert Huth, who can believe we are interested in another centre-back? Rio is an amazing player, we can't hide that, but this season John Terry is the best central defender in England.'

On links to buying Rio Ferdinand.

'Lampard is great. The way he plays is the way he trains, so his motivation to play is his motivation to train. He's a strong boy mentally and physically and if he steers clear of injuries and suspensions he could set a record that is impossible to catch. It's unlikely he will get banned because he's such a fair player.'

Mourinho praises Frank Lampard after he broke the record for the most consecutive games played for Chelsea.

'I really don't want to think about him. The best way to face an injury from a very important player is to forget him, I don't speak to him. He is in the medical department and, when they tell me he's ready to start working with the coaching staff, we will welcome him with open arms. When my fitness coach says he's ready to play, I will jump for joy. But at the moment, he cannot play, so I do not think about him. I have to work with the other players, to support and motivate them. I'll never use Arjen Robben as an excuse for anything.'

When injured, players are out of sight, out of mind for Mourinho . . .

'The club bought him to be ready to play football and now he will be out of competition for a long period. The first one to break the relationship was the player so he cannot complain.'

The Mutu saga dragged on . . .

'I cannot say be patient to players because if I was in their position, I may not be able to be patient. That is football at the highest level. If a player wants to be the king of the club, he wants to play sixty matches a season and he wants to always be in the team, he has to join a small club.'

Mourinho explains the perils of squad rotation.

'Didier [Drogba] knows I always like my team to be a team from the moment we leave London until we arrive home and I want every single player after the match to go home with the team. When I brought him off before the end he was laughing and asking me if he'd done enough to stay on. Everyone thinks I am dreadful and never open to communication.'

After allowing Drogba to stay on in Paris to collect his Marc-Vivien Foe award after the game against Paris Saint Germain.

'I wouldn't like him. He is a very good player, but in England you cannot play in midfield with two players who are 1.70m. With Claude Makelele, it would not be a good combination.'

On Edgar Davids, with whom he had been linked.

'He is a Liverpool boy and decided to stay at home. I too was faced with that decision. I had to choose between staying at Porto and moving to Chelsea and chose Chelsea because I wanted a new life. I wish Steven good success this season but hope he finishes below us in the league.'

On Steven Gerrard's on/off move to Chelsea, July 2004.

'I'm a great defender of team spirit and teamwork and the first thing I have to promise to my new players is that I will look at them all with the same eyes. I don't want special relations with one of them. I hate to speak about individuals. Players don't win you trophies, teams win trophies, squads win trophies. I cannot say I love this player, but generally I love the players who love to win. Not only the ones that love to win in 90 minutes but love to win every day, in every training session and in all of their lives.'

Mourinho on his selection process.

'Frank is one of the best players in the world and not just because he is one of my players. He's really strong physically and mentally. It's a wonderful record, especially because midfielders run much more than defenders or attackers. Lamps puts in something like twelve and half, thirteen kilometres each match. If you multiply that by 114 matches it's a big engine, and a special car.'

More praise for Frank Lampard.

Ferguson, Wenger and the Rest: Mourinho on Managers and Coaches

If rivalries are essential to sport, they are fundamental to football. While one would never claim that the passion that drives the competition between, say, Real Madrid and Barcelona, Celtic and Rangers, or England and Scotland, is the same as those between managers, it is fair to say that the war of words between Sir Alex Ferguson and Arsène Wenger has been one of the most intriguing battles to have emerged from the Premiership. For years they have been sparring, psyching each other out and creating an atmosphere that suggested the Premiership was theirs and theirs alone. It seemed no one could compete with them, no one could take them on and actually win. Then Mourinho appeared ...

It's uncertain how much of Mourinho's initial statements were designed to get under the skin of both Wenger and Ferguson, however it certainly deflected attention from the team and onto the manager. When Ferguson wryly pointed out that Mourinho's entrance was rather like having a new gunslinger in town he was right on the money. Mourinho had come to upset the status quo and give Wenger and Ferguson someone else to deal with.

Funnily enough, Mourinho seemed to use the same tactics in post-match interviews as the old guard. Questioning referees for not seeing incidents, trying to unsettle opponents before the game, wondering aloud if there were forces at work which were conspiring against his team – all of these had been used before by Wenger and Ferguson. The difference was that Mourinho could not only dish it out, but he could take it too, often turning it to his advantage. There are some great quotes here in response to something that someone from United or Arsenal had said, and it seems that no matter what comes Mourinho's way, he would make the very best use of it.

This approach suddenly made the personal feud between United and Arsenal seem a little less important. At some points in the season it felt like they were going through the motions while trying to work out what they were going to do with this Portuguese upstart. They didn't come up with an answer during the season, and it was only perhaps the quiet, self-effacing form of Rafa Benitez who came anywhere close to a draw with Mourinho's mouth – and it took him until the Champions' League final ...

As Peter Kenyon said on Mourinho's appointment, 'He represents the new generation of football coaches.' It is perhaps this that truly scares Wenger, Ferguson and the rest.

'He felt he [Ferguson] could maybe put some pressure on us. I understood it. I work my players and I work the press conference to try to put a good atmosphere around my team. We play, we won, finish, shake hands. That's it. For me, no fight, no problem.'

After the mind-games of the Manchester United-Porto game, Mourinho explains how to use the press conference to your advantage.

'I agree money doesn't buy points and victories. If you go back a few months, Porto, with 10 per cent of Manchester United's budget, beat them. So he's absolutely correct. Money buys players but not a team.'

A perfect rejoinder to Sir Alex's grumblings about the Abramovich billions.

'I hope that we have many, many rounds because if you have many rounds it means Sir Alex still feels young and stays at Manchester United and it means that my work is going well and I stay here for many seasons. I hope we have ten rounds, fifteen rounds — just until the last whistle.'

Mourinho appears to like his new sparring partner.

'There is nothing against Sir Alex whatsoever. After the game on Wednesday we were together in my office and we spoke and drank wine. Unfortunately it was a very bad bottle of wine and he was complaining, so when we go to Old Trafford for the second leg, on my birthday, I will take a beautiful bottle of Portuguese wine.'

Catering at the Chelsea Village was not to Sir Alex's rarefied tastes.

'Maybe when I'm 60, have been in the same league for twenty years and I know everybody and everybody respects me a lot; maybe one day I will have this power to speak and people tremble a little bit.'

José suggests that Neale Barry was softened by Sir Alex after the game Manchester United in January. This was one of the more subtle comments made in the aftermath of the match, the others landed Mourinho in hot water with the footballing authorities – again.

'I don't know him well, so I think it's not fair to speak about someone I don't know personally. When he says he likes other Chelsea teams much more than our team I know why – because we are the champions. He preferred the other way when they were the champions. I didn't like Arsenal at the start of the season when they smashed everybody and I don't like them now when they beat Everton 7–0 and they win. But I liked them very much in the middle of the season when every weekend they lost points. I was in love with them then, so I can understand why Arsène doesn't like us.'

On Arsène Wenger.

'I respect him, but not just respect, I like him. He is a person to fight with but a person that when a game ends we share a glass of wine and speak openly. He is a very correct person and he teaches me a few things.'

On Sir Alex Ferguson.

'I shook hands with him before the game two or three times. When the game finished I went onto the pitch with my players. I think this is ridiculous, the game has finished, I'm happy, I want to be with my players, I don't want to be with other people.'

After allegations he didn't shake Mark Hughes' hand after playing Blackburn in February 2005.

'Actually I don't care.'

Paul Sturrock's early exit from Southampton doesn't really register on Mourinho's radar.

'The best job in the world is to be a sacked coach. You get up at 10.30 a.m., take breakfast, go for a jog, followed by a sauna and a calm surf of sporting sites on the net. Followed by lunch, a siesta and then a meeting with your stockbroker or accountant. Return home, have a great meal with the family. That still leaves you time to criticise people you don't know. There are so many coaches in this world who want to work but can't and there are those dashing blades who, through their quality and prestige, could work but don't want to, because life as a parasite fulfils them professionally and economically. Get to work, you idle scoundrel. And if you don't want to, let others work in peace.'

Mourinho rounds on former managers who have dared to criticise him.

'I heard that and I suggest if one of you is Mr Ranieri's friend or has his number you should call him and explain to him that for a team to win the European Cup it has to beat many teams from many countries. I did not win the cup playing against twenty Portuguese teams. I played and beat a team from his own country, Italy, from your country and the one he was working in, England.'

Talking of former managers . . . Mourinho responds to Claudio Ranieri's comments that he would struggle.

'People want a storm but there isn't one. There's no problem and no war or mind-games between us. I respect Sir Alex a lot because he's a great manager, but he must follow the procedure, we must all be the same. I'm a European champion and so is Ferguson, it doesn't matter who you are. I don't speak with referees and I don't want other managers doing it, it's the rule. One thing is to speak, one thing is to shout.'

Mourinho deflects *any* hint of gamesmanship between himself and Sir Alex in January 2005.

'I've been to the UEFA meetings for the last three or four years and have met them both. We all know each other but they have a very good relationship and respect each other. They are good friends. They have dined at the same table and spoken about football. In the last two years at these meetings I have been in the same group as them and they have talked about football and shared their opinions. But when the big game arrives one of them is the boss of his ship and vice-versa.'

And even suggests that Ferguson and Wenger see eye to eye occasionally . . .

The Law: Mourinho on Referees, the FA and Other Nuisances

Before a ball had been kicked in anger in the 2005–6 Premiership season, a debate was already raging about managers criticising referees. New rules made it an offence to make comments about a referee before or after a game. Quite how managers will cope with this is difficult to say, though it will certainly make Mourinho's after-game comments a little less fiery.

In the wake of the Anders Frisk affair, where allegations and counter-allegations flew about as to whether there had been contact between Frisk and Barcelona manager Frank Rijkaard, it seemed that criticising the referee had become more than just a way of letting off some steam. The ramifications were steep for Mourinho, who was banned from joining his team for two games, but it also quite eloquently expressed José's problems with the footballing establishment.

Of course, he is not the only manager to fall foul of comments made in the heat of the moment, but even by Premiership standards he has been on the wrong end of disciplinary proceedings an awful lot. Sometimes it seems he simply cannot help it – the comments against the linesman who gave Liverpool's goal in the Champions' League semi-final, for example, were met with howls of protest from UEFA who had fined him for criticising the refereeing in the previous round.

The thing is that moaning about decisions going against you is part of being a football fan. Some of Mourinho's comments have been harsh — in some cases perhaps unfair — but some have been witty and have only managed to ingratiate him further to the fans. While he might have to be careful whom he criticises, it will be a boring season if he keeps his mouth shut for the whole 38 games.

'If I made a mistake then I apologise. I am happy that I'm not going to jail because of that.'

In penitent mood following the finger-to-lip gesture to the Liverpool fans during the Carling Cup final.

'Of course it was a penalty. In some countries you get two penalties for that offence.'

Rob Styles comes in for some stick after booking Drogba for diving rather than giving a penalty against Aston Villa.

'The referee was inefficient. It was an adulterated result.'

One of his more innocuous comments after the 2–1 defeat by Barcelona.

'If I say what I feel in my soul, I will attract more headlines and more trouble. It is strange that in this industry, when you say what you feel and believe, you pay for it. My message to the press is this: please concentrate on the pitch tonight. You don't have to try and find me, you can't.'

Responding to the question of where he would watch the quarter-final against Bayern Munich, for which he was suspended.

'In the games between Portugal and Greece and England and Croatia, Collina was the best player on the pitch . . . Maybe it's an exaggeration, but I say give him the *Ballon d'Or* for being the best professional in Europe.'

A compliment to the Italian ref, or a slating of his own nation and his soon-to-be adopted one?

'There was a ridiculous pursuit based on a false notion. The notes that were circulating were ones we had prepared before the game . . . The assistants were organised, prepared. They were communicating amongst themselves.'

On whether there had been communication with his assistants when suspended from the quarter-finals.

'I'm not on the bench on Wednesday, and also next week, and it's something that I don't want to comment or say what I have in myself. It's clear you cannot say too much. I must keep quiet.'

After being banned after comments about Anders Frisk.

'Because I am loyal to my people, because I believe what my people say to me, I am involved in something I don't want. But I cannot run away from it because I always trust my people.'

José explains how he came to be banned by UEFA.

'Mr Roth has two ways out, apologise or it goes to court.'

Mourinho gets litigious with Volker Roth, the UEFA head of refereeing, after he accused him of being an 'enemy of football'.

'It's a shame that Frisk has decided to leave football. If this decision is linked to the criticism of his performance in the Barcelona game, it seems strange to me. There's similar criticism every day, all around the world, for managers, directors and players. It's a normal situation. If there are other motives I do not know them and would like them to be known.'

UEFA later dismissed links between Mourinho's comments and the retirement of Anders Frisk.

'I am more than unhappy. Unhappy is a nice word because I cannot say the word I have in my heart or in my soul. I don't want to speak about it because if I do, maybe I will have to go to the FA or pay out some money instead of spending it on Christmas gifts.'

Mourinho rails against Thierry Henry's controversial quickly taken free-kick goal in the December 2004 clash between Chelsea and Arsenal.

'We lost and that's reality. I thought it was impossible for the referee to see the penalty incident because he was fifty metres away. You are not happy because a decision is given against you, but I am not the type of person that likes to pressure referees like others do.'

After defeat by Manchester City, October 2004.

'They [Arsenal] always seem to have two or three days' rest in which to recover. Perhaps it's something to do with the television schedule. All my players are tired, especially John Terry.'

Mourinho spies a conspiracy . . .

'I would like somebody to tell me who is controlling these dates and times because I cannot understand why we always get the most difficult fixture list.'

And again . . .

'After the first five games of next season's Champions' League we have to play away while Arsenal are at home . . . Why are different clubs treated in different ways?'

And one last time. Sir Alex jokingly agreed with him, though the statistics didn't quite bear him out.

'The man of the match was the referee because of that decision and he cost us the points. We should have had a penalty and three points. It is ridiculous. If a similar situation happens with Thierry Henry or Ruud van Nistelrooy we will see if a similar decision is given. I do not believe it will.'

After Rob Styles didn't give a penalty for a foul on Didier Drogba in a game against Aston Villa in September 2004.

The Future:
2005–6 and Beyond

So where does José Mourinho go from here? Already he
has announced that he will only stay at Chelsea for the
length of his contract – at the longest – giving him just
five or six seasons to continue his magic at Stamford
Bridge. It's certain, and he has admitted himself, that he
will not end up as decorated as Sir Alex Ferguson, but if
that first amazing season is anything to go by, Mourinho
will surely become a Premiership legend.

Obviously the target for the immediate future is to retain the
Premiership, a feat that only Manchester United have managed
over the years. Mourinho's desire to dominate the home game
is clear to see and, judging by his comments about the
difficulty of winning the Premiership versus that of winning the
Champions' League, it is the 38 games of the Premiership that
are the most important to him. Though it seems unlikely he'd
turn up his nose at being European Champion again ...

Beyond that, it's anyone's guess. As Mourinho himself
points out, a run of bad results could see him being
unceremoniously flung out of Chelsea – but this seems
highly unlikely. The bookmakers – who rarely get these
things very wrong – cite only Arsène Wenger as safer
from the sack in 2005–6. Mourinho looks like he's staying
put and will relish the challenge of wresting entire control
of the Premiership from Arsenal and Manchester United.
It won't be easy, but if anyone can do it, you'd bet it would
be José Mourinho.

'You want to win everything but normally you cannot do it. It's almost impossible in modern football. We can win two of the four trophies. If we win the Premiership or the Champions' League – or win both cups – it will not be a failure. If I win nothing? I don't know what I would do. One day it will happen and I will have to cope with it.'

Content only with more victories, Mourinho wonders what a trophyless season would feel like.

'Three are leaving, three are coming in. We're going to bring in a left-back, a midfielder and a centre-forward ... But there will be no Portuguese players coming in.'

José articulates his plans for new signings for the 2005–6 season – before they were blighted.

'We started thinking about the next campaign a few months ago. It's easy to prepare for next season as we have a group of champions and want to keep them.'

Thinking ahead in May 2005.

'I will look forward to seeing the first pre-season training session on 6 July. I will be coaching and watching and seeing what we have for the future. In such an important league you don't fail if you don't win the league but in my five years if I don't win the championship once or twice more I'd say we don't have a really great team.'

Looking forward to his legacy, June 2005.

'Chelsea in the future won't need this kind of budget. I'll bet that in the last year of my five-year deal we won't buy a player. Next season, we'll buy maybe two or three; the season after, one or two. The next season we'll buy one and after that we won't need any.'

Talking transfers, July 2005.

'In this moment people have seen Chelsea play Milan with two teams and you couldn't say at this moment which is the better one ... I asked the staff, "If we play tomorrow against Wigan, what is your first eleven?" There were four different answers and they were all different from me. I will wait fifteen days before I decide. We have one of the best squads in Europe. I don't know which team is the second one.'

Mourinho reveals the difficulty of having to decide from two teams, July 2005.

'For me it's hard because I feel everybody deserves to play and that's a problem. Players have to understand the quality of our squad and that it will be hard for them to have a place. But I would say some will play a maximum of 70 per cent of the matches so it means that some of the players will get 30 per cent.'

Mourinho gives some of his players a boost before the season starts . . .

'There are no untouchables. I am not untouchable. Maybe if I lose three or four consecutive games next season and go out of two cup competitions, I will find myself back in Portugal. The only untouchable thing is the club. I respect what players have done in the past. But what is important is the future, not the past. If Terry's form declines, we have Ricardo Carvalho, William Gallas and Robert Huth. I would not hesitate to drop a player if his form drops and the players know that.'

. . . but also issues a warning.

'If I'm here for five years, working without any big problems and going about my job in a normal way, then I think a big club like Chelsea have to win the Champions' League. It is possible we can win it this year. With the group of players we have, we can be strong in both competitions. To guarantee the Champions' League, we would need to control factors that are beyond our control. If you were to ask me whether I needed something extra in my squad to adapt it completely to my needs I would like to have one more midfield player.'

Mourinho sets his target on the Champions' League, July 2005.

'If a player asked me for a rest, I would say: "You can rest for the World Cup for the next three months and you can go to Soho Square for your wages."'

The World Cup is clearly seen as some kind of nuisance by Mourinho.

'It's not difficult to keep and maintain the motivation. They are English champions and they now know the different feelings that go with that and they want to keep that winning feeling.'

Mourinho hopes for a continuation of Chelsea's winning ways, July 2005.

'I told the players on the first day of pre-season to forget about the World Cup. If they think too much about the World Cup they're in danger because they forget Chelsea. They shouldn't think about it. They should think about training every day to the maximum of their potential for the club. The competition is very hard here and if they think about other things they're in trouble. But if at the end of the season I go on my holidays and all my players go to Germany I will be the proudest man.'

Mourinho reiterates the importance of ignoring the World Cup.

'I'm looking forward to seeing the fight. Getting into the team is their problem, not mine. In pre-season everyone will get the same chance, 45 minutes each, then maybe 60 and 30 minutes. They will get the same chances to play but they must prove they should be in the team. I'm not stupid, all I care about is winning.'

On the competition for places, July 2005.

'We have still a space in midfield. It is an area where we don't have problems, we are not in trouble – but we have a space, so during the open market if we have the chance to get a good player we will do it.'

On the on-off struggle to sign Michael Essien.

'With Shaun, Cole, Arjen and Damien, we have a fantastic group of wingers to compete and give us the best every other match. And with Shaun, we will not have the kind of problems like we had last season when Robben and Duff were both injured. This season, with the World Cup next summer, there will be a lot of friendlies. And as we will be in five competitions, we need this balance like we have in every other position. I am very happy.'

Contented with his squad, July 2005.

'I will always say what I feel about facts, but if I am asked to make a comment or give an opinion or analysis of a problem, I have to cool down and really think twice before saying something. But facts are facts, facts are not controversy.'

Can it really be so? Will Mourinho keep his mouth shut in 2006? We certainly hope not . . .

'My idea is to work for thirteen more years. I want to spend four of them with the Portuguese national team. When I say four, I say two, you know – the European Cup and the World Cup or just the World Cup. So, before that period of two or four years, I have eleven or nine years in front of me. In these eleven or nine years, I see me in English football, yes.'

Planning for the future, Mourinho style.

A Note on Sources

In compiling this book, I have attempted to include only public statements made by José Mourinho and tried to avoid any exclusive interview quotes.

The quotes have been taken from a variety of local, national and international newspapers, as well as from some Internet sources – most notably the excellent BBC Sport website (http://news.BBCSport.co.uk/sport/).

Also helpful on Mourinho's background – and one of the best pieces on Mourinho yet written – was Mark Honigsbaum's long article in the *Observer Sports Monthly*, 1 August 2004

J.A.
August 2005

Sources

B.C.: Before Chelsea:
Gavin Berry, *Sunday Mail*, 27 April 2003
Daily Record, 15 May 2003
Gavin Berry, *Sunday Mail*, 27 April 2003
Graeme Bryce, *News of the World*, 18 May 2003
BBC Sport website, 21 May 2003
BBC Sport website, 20 May 2003
Tim Gordon, *Mirror*, 16 May 2003
Ewing Graham, *Glasgow Herald*, 21 May 2003
Daily Record, 22 May 2003
Christopher Davis, *Daily Telegraph*, 23 May 2003
Michael Baillie, *Mirror*, 16 March 2004
BBC Sport website, 21 April 2004
Iain Campbell, *Mirror*, 23 May 2003
Martin Roberts, *Independent*, 23 May 2003
Bill Edgar, *The Times*, 20 February 2004
Paul McCarthy, *Sunday People*, 29 February 2004
Martin Lipton, *Mirror*, 14 January 2005
Eric Beauchamp, *Sun*, 27 February 2004
Sun, 1 March 2004
Evening Chronicle, 10 March 2004
BBC Sport website, 5 May 2004
Dave Faulkner, *Time Out*, 23 February 2005

The Special One: Mourinho on Himself
Mark Honigsbaum, *Observer*, 1 August 2004
Russell Kempson, *The Times*, 21 August 2004
Mark Honigsbaum, *Observer*, 1 August 2004
Mirror, 23 August 2004

Newcastle Journal, 21 August 2004
Independent, 2 October 2004
Independent, 19 February 2005
Michelle Kaufman, *Miami Herald*, 27 February 2005
Guardian, 11 March 2005
James Lawton, *Independent*, 1 January 2005
Irish Times, 11 April 2005
BBC Sport website, 22 October 2004
Daily Star, 2 April 2005
David Harrison, *News of the World*, 3 April 2005
Independent, 7 May 2005
BBC Sport website, 2 June 2004
ibid
Christopher Davis, *Daily Telegraph*, 19 May 2005
BBC Sport website, 4 July 2005
BBC Sport website, 26 September 2004
Mark Honigsbaum, *Observer*, 1 August 2004
BBC Sport website, 5 September 2004

At Home: The Premiership 2004–5

Joe Lovejoy, *Sunday Times*, 23 May 2004
BBC Sport website, 30 November 2004
Tim Nichols, *Daily Mail*, 1 March 2005
Daniel King, *Daily Mail*, 11 July 2004
Ravi Ubha, *Seattle Post Intelligencer*, 8 June 2004
Mark Honigsbaum, *Observer*, 1 August 2004
BBC Sport website, 26 December 2004
David Randall, *Independent on Sunday*, 27 February 2005
Mark Honigsbaum, *Observer*, 1 August 2004
Independent, 21 August 2004
Ken Dyer, *Evening Standard*, 23 August 2004
Martin Lipton, *Mirror*, 8 November 2004
Andrew Dillon, *Sun*, 29 March 2005
BBC Sport website, 17 February 2005
BBC Sport website, 6 June 2004
BBC Sport website, 21 August 2004

SOURCES

Birmingham Post, 25 September 2004
Mark Fleming, *Daily Express*, 2 May 2005
Dominic Fifield, *Guardian*, 27 January 2005
Jim Keat, *News of the World*, 27 February 2005
Independent, 25 September 2004
Matt Hughes, *Evening Standard*, 22 November 2004
Independent, 5 February 2005
Tim Nichols, *Daily Mail*, 11 February 2005
Gary Jacob, *The Times*, 26 May 2005
ibid.
BBC Sport website, 25 July 2004
BBC Sport website, 4 June 2005
BBC Sport website, 4 May 2005
Matt Hughes, *Evening Standard*, 3 June 2005
BBC Sport website, 21 February 2005
BBC Sport website, 26 December 2004
BBC Sport website, 19 January 2005
BBC Sport website, 31 December 2004
BBC Sport website, 2 December 2004
BBC Sport website, 24 December 2004
Christopher Davis, *Daily Telegraph*, 19 May 2005
Andrew Dillon, *Sun*, 29 March 2005
Mark Fleming, *Daily Express*, 2 May 2005
BBC Sport website, 11 May 2005
BBC Sport website, 6 May 2005
BBC Sport website, 7 May 2005
BBC Sport website, 19 July 2005
BBC Sport website, 12 July 2005
BBC Sport website, 7 May 2005

Playing Away: The Champions' League 2004–5
John Rawling, *Guardian*, 27 September 2004
Independent, 2 October 2004
BBC Sport website, 20 October 2004
BBC Sport website, 2 November 2004
BBC Sport website, 2 September 2004

BBC Sport website, 8 March 2005
John Carlin, *Independent*, 23 February 2005
BBC Sport website, 17 December 2004
Guardian Unlimited, 11 April 2005
Steve Tongue, *Independent on Sunday*, 10 April 2005
Western Daily Press, 27 April 2005
Independent, 1 May 2005
Irish News, 28 April 2005
BBC Sport website, 6 May 2005
Phil Thomas, *Sun*, 4 May 2005
BBC Sport website, 4 May 2005
Peter Edwards, *Daily Express*, 25 July 2005
Jason Burt, *Independent*, 18 December 2004
Ian McGarry, *Daily Mail*, 25 July 2005

José's Way: Mourinho's Philosophy of Football
Jim Holden, *Sunday Express*, 18 April 2004
Mark Honigsbaum, *Observer*, 1 August 2004
Matt Scott, *Guardian*, 18 September 2004
Mark Honigsbaum, *Observer*, 1 August 2004
Nick Townsend, *Independent on Sunday*, 3 October 2004
BBC Sport website, 25 January 2005
Sun, 15 November 2004
Nick Szczepanik, *The Times*, 8 December 2004
Richard Williams, *Guardian*, 3 January 2005
Martin Lipton, *Mirror*, 8 November 2004
Evening Chronicle, 29 December 2004
Jason Burt, *Independent*, 18 December 2004
Iain Burchell, *Daily Star*, 24 January 2005
Liverpool Daily Post, 21 February 2005
BBC Sport website, 2 June 2004
Guardian, 11 March 2005
Andrew Dillon, *Sun*, 29 March 2005
Russell Kempson, *The Times*, 7 May 2005
BBC Sport website, 23 August 2004
John Rawling, *Guardian*, 27 September 2004

SOURCES

Matt Hughes, *Evening Standard*, 22 November 2004
Mark Honigsbaum, *Observer*, 1 August 2004
Andrew Dillon, *Sun*, 26 May 2005
Jim Keat, *News of the World*, 2 May 2004
ibid.
Luke Gossett, *Sunday Mirror*, 18 May 2003
Ian Hawkey, *Sunday Times*, 18 May 2003
BBC Sport website, 4 July 2005

The Players: Mourinho on his Own and Others
Matt Scott, *Guardian*, 6 July 2004
Damien Fletcher, *Mirror*, 10 July 2004
Ronald Atkin, *Independent on Sunday*, 11 July 2004
Danny Fullbrook, *Daily Star*, 25 October 2004
Mark Honigsbaum, *Observer*, 1 August 2004
Mark Fleming, *Daily Express*, 2 May 2005
Jason Burt, *Independent*, 18 December 2004
Daily Express, 25 October 2004
Gary Jacob, *The Times*, 26 May 2005
BBC Sport website, 22 April 2005
BBC Sport website, 18 December 2004
BBC Sport website, 20 February 2005
BBC Sport website, 30 October 2004
BBC Sport website, 15 October 2004
BBC Sport website, 14 September 2004
BBC Sport website, 5 July 2004
Matt Scott, *Guardian*, 6 July 2004
BBC Sport website, 2 June 2004
Matt Scott, *Guardian*, 18 September 2004

Ferguson, Wenger and the Rest: Mourinho on Managers and Coaches
Mark Honigsbaum, *Observer*, 1 August 2004
Mirror, 23 August 2004
Mark Honigsbaum, *Observer*, 1 August 2004
BBC Sport website, 14 January 2005

David Woods, *Daily Star*, 14 January 2005
Andrew Warshaw, *Sunday Telegraph*, 5 June 2005
BBC Sport website, 20 May 2005
ibid
BBC Sport website, 1 February 2005
Mirror, 20 September 2004
Simon Pia, *The Scotsman*, 12 April 2005
BBC Sport website, 2 June 2004
BBC Sport website, 14 January 2005
BBC Sport website, 23 October 2004

The Law: Referees, UEFA and Other Nuisances
Coventry Evening Telegraph, 5 March 2005
Chick Young, *Daily Star*, 22 January 2005
Patrick McCurdy, *Sunday Mirror*, 27 February 2005
Michael Walker, *Guardian*, 7 April 2005
The Times, 25 June 2004
Chris Maume, *Independent*, 20 April 2005
BBC Sport website, 4 April 2005
BBC Sport website, 29 March 2005
BBC Sport website, 16 March 2005
ibid
BBC Sport website, 13 December 2004
BBC Sport website, 16 October 2004
BBC Sport website, 29 December 2004
Dave Kidd, *Sun*, 25 February 2005
Guardian Unlimited, 13 July 2005
BBC Sport website, 11 September 2004

The Future: 2005–6 and Beyond
Daniel King, *Mail on Sunday*, 17 July 2005
Associated Press Worldstream, 2 June 2005
BBC Sport website, 17 May 2005
BBC Sport website, 11 May 2005
BBC Sport website, 4 July 2005
Simon Johnson, *Independent*, 28 July 2005

SOURCES

Richard Bright, *Daily Telegraph*, 26 July 2005
Daniel King, *Mail on Sunday*, 24 July 2005
Ian McGarry, *Daily Mail*, 25 July 2005
Rob Beasley, *News of the World*, 24 July 2005
ibid
Matt Hughes, *Evening Standard*, 21 July 2005
Andrew Dillon, *Sun*, 21 July 2005
Evening Mail, 18 July 2005
Matt Hughes, *Evening Standard*, 18 July 2005
Ronald Atkin, *Independent on Sunday*, 17 July 2005
Mary Hannigan, *Irish Times*, 4 April 2005